WEDGWOOD JASPER WARE

John Bedford

WALKER AND COMPANY
NEW YORK

Library of Congress Catalog Card Number 65–22130

First published in the United States of America in
1965 by Walker and Company, a division of
Publications Development Corporation
Third Printing 1968

Printed in Hong Kong

Contents

INTRODUCTION   4

1. JOSIAH WEDGWOOD, MASTER
       POTTER   5

2. THE MAKING OF JASPER WARE   10

3. DECORATIVE AND ORNAMENTAL   18

4. TEA AND TABLE WARE   34

5. TOILETTE AND TRINKETS   40

6. CAMEOS AND MEDALLIONS   44

7. MARKS ON JASPER WARE   60

Introduction

For nearly two hundred years now people have been enjoying jasper ware. 'Wedgwood blue', as a colour, has passed into the language, and the wares invented by Josiah Wedgwood at Etruria in the 1770s still come from his descendants' new factory at Barlaston. They have found their way into most civilized countries; they have been imitated in all kinds of materials; and of course they are collected everywhere.

Whole libraries of works have been written on Staffordshire's most famous master potter and his many and varied products, but I do not know of one entirely devoted to jasper ware. Hence this little book, which is offered to anyone who has a few pieces, and wishes to know more about them, or perhaps would like to go further and join the band of jasper ware collectors. It gives the story of the man who developed the ware, what was made in it, and something about the subjects of the famous white reliefs.

As expressed at Etruria by Josiah Wedgwood's band of designers and modellers, the neo-classical styles of the late eighteenth century come out mostly in a softened, sweetened, almost domesticated English version which could only have appeared at the time and place it did. Compared with other ware of the same quality, and rarity, jasper must be considered undervalued at today's prices: so no better time could be chosen to start collecting.

It remains to express one's grateful thanks to such helpful sources of information and illustrations as Moira Gibson, of Josiah Wedgwood & Sons Ltd; Harry M. Buten, of the Buten Museum of Wedgwood, Merion (Pennsylvania); and the staff of the Victoria and Albert Museum, London.

1. Josiah Wedgwood, Master Potter

Josiah Wedgwood, the inventor of jasper ware, came from a family which had been making pots around the country lanes of Burslem and Stoke since Elizabethan days. He was christened at Burslem on 12th July 1730, the twelfth and youngest son of Thomas and Mary Wedgwood, of the Churchyard Pottery.

His great-great-grandfather Gilbert, also a master potter, inherited an estate of two hundred acres through his wife. But by the time Josiah's father died, leaving the Churchyard Pottery to his eldest son Thomas, there was little of the family fortune left. Josiah, then aged nine, was left twenty pounds—although in fact there was not enough money in the estate to pay even this tiny legacy.

So he was put to work at the family pottery under his brother Thomas, and five years later was apprenticed to learn the 'Art, Mistery, Occupation or Imployment of Throwing and Handleing'. When he had served his time he did not stay on with his brother as journeyman but went out to work, first for a potter at Cliffe Bank, then, in 1754, for the great Thomas Whieldon.

After Wedgwood himself, Whieldon is probably the next most famous name in the history of the Staffordshire potteries. At the time Josiah joined him he was making the traditional Staffordshire wares—the saltglazes, the mottled, agate and marbled stonewares, the black and colour glazed earthenwares—with outstanding craftsmanship and individuality.

All these wares are now highly prized by collectors: but at that time, as it appears from Josiah's later correspondence, they were going through the doldrums. The early creamware and the saltglazed and agate stonewares, so attractive to modern taste, had been in the market a long time without improvement; they were also being outsold by the enamelled white Chinese and Continental porcelains which were being imported into England in huge quantities.

But Josiah saw great possibilities for improvement in the colour glazed earthenware with which Whieldon and other Staffordshire men were trying to emulate the richly coloured glazed types of porcelains from China, many of them with applied decoration or in the shapes of fruits and vegetables. Wedgwood began to experiment with glazes of his own. He also showed a good business instinct by coming to an arrangement whereby he would let his master have the benefit of his discoveries but was under no obligation to disclose the secret of their making.

By the year 1759 Josiah's work in this field was sufficiently advanced to justify his setting up on his own as a master potter. For ten pounds a year he rented from wealthier relatives the Ivy House Works in Burslem. Here he worked out one of the earliest of his many inventions—the famous green glaze still popular today. It appeared on cauliflower and pineapple teapots and jugs, on leaf-shaped plates and dishes and many other wares.

His next great invention was an improved version of

View of Etruria. (From a print in The Story of Wedgwood *by Alison Kelly.)*

the traditional Staffordshire creamwares, which developed after moving to the Bell Works—so called because the workers were summoned by a bell instead of the customary horn.

Josiah Wedgwood.

This new and highly efficient and practical ware—which earned him Royal patronage, and the name 'Queen's Ware' for his product—set him on the way to a fortune. It enabled him to introduce mass-production methods and revolutionized the production of table ware throughout Europe. There followed, one after another, his other contributions to the potters' art—including at first a terracotta called rosso antico, black basaltes, a more elegant use of the marbling techniques, and cane ware—best known in the form of the famous pie-dishes.

WEDGWOOD AND BENTLEY

Then Josiah met a man who was to change his entire outlook on life. He was on a journey to Liverpool, whither many of his wares were sent by packhorse for decoration by transfer printing, when he was suddenly struck down by trouble with his leg, a legacy from a childhood attack of smallpox; ultimately the limb was amputated. The surgeon who attended him in Liverpool introduced him to a local merchant named Thomas Bentley, a widely travelled man of taste and learning who was closely in touch with the contemporary wave of enthusiasm for reviving classical styles. This had been largely touched off by the works of art found in the diggings at the buried Roman cities of Pompeii and Herculaneum.

7

The two men became intimate friends and corresponded with each other continuously: Wedgwood's letters to Bentley have been preserved in quantity but Bentley's replies have for the most part disappeared. Some say they were destroyed by Sarah Wedgwood, Josiah's wife, in a fit of jealousy.

ETRURIA REBORN

The outcome of the meeting was that the two men set up in business together to make 'ornamental wares'—as distinct from the 'useful wares' which Josiah was already making at the time. In 1768 they bought land about two miles outside Burslem and built there not only a new pottery and a house for its master, but an entire village for the workers. They called it Etruria, after the newly discovered Greek vases—by an archaeological error they were thought to be Etruscan in origin.

Here it was that the Wedgwood family continued their business right down to the year 1940, when once more they moved out and built a new pottery in the country, this time at Barlaston outside Stoke. But if you go to the potteries today you will still find the district of Etruria, together with a few of the buildings that the first Josiah built there.

The new styles were first expressed in the marbled wares and the black basaltes—Josiah's development of the unglazed blackwares long made in Staffordshire by the peasant potters. At the factory's opening in 1760, with Bentley operating the wheel, Wedgwood himself threw and turned six such vases, to be painted in encaustic colours with classical figures. These 'First-Day' vases were all inscribed 'Artes Etruriae Renascuntur'—'The Arts of Etruria are Reborn' and one of them is still to be seen in the Wedgwood Museum at Barlaston.

THE FIRST JASPER

But Josiah wanted to offer reproductions of the Greco-Roman gems of polished stone or coloured glass with relief

8

carving. For this he needed a white stoneware of great fineness, capable of being tinted to any required colour and hard enough to be polished like a stone on the lapidary's wheel.

Throughout 1773 and 1774 he tried different clays and earths under all kinds of conditions. Eventually he found what he wanted in Derbyshire; it was a sulphate of barium associated with the lead ore mined there, and known locally as Derbyshire 'cawk'. By the next year he had under reasonable control what he called 'a fine white terra cotta'. This was not what we know as the jasper ware body today, but a material with a smooth waxen surface. Cameos made of it were in high relief and looked like ivory carvings—according to Rathbone, the late-nineteenth-century collector and dealer, workmen at Etruria would say: 'Old Josiah used to put butter in his paste when he made these early medallions.' The ground was often coloured by hand, the rarest being the black, of which only eight examples are known.

Then, after infinite trouble with firing and colouring what Josiah called his 'whimsical jasper', he hit upon the real formula. The mixture was, according to Sir Arthur Church: sulphate of barium 59 parts; clay 29 parts; flint 10 parts; carbonate of barium 2 parts.

In the autumn of 1776 Josiah wrote again to Bentley announcing final success. He had produced, in his own words, 'a fine white artificial jasper, of exquisite beauty and delicacy, proper for cameos, portraits and bas reliefs'. It was capable, in the words of a catalogue published later, 'of receiving colours through its whole surface, in a manner which no other body, ancient or modern, has been known to do. This makes it particularly fit for cameos, portraits and all subjects in bas reliefs; as the ground may be made of any colour throughout, without paint or enamel, and the raised figures of a pure white.'

Jasper ware was born and had started off on the first of its centuries.

2. The Making of Jasper Ware

Without its relief decoration, jasper would be but another coloured stoneware. So let us look at these decorations more closely.

There is no mystery about them, for they are being made by Wedgwood at Barlaston today exactly as they were in the 1770s at Etruria. Clay of the same material as the piece to be decorated, but without a staining oxide in it, is pressed into 'pitcher' moulds. These moulds, of course, are in 'intaglio', that is, the design is sunken below the surface, so that when the piece of clay comes out it is in 'relief', that is, it stands above the surface.

Any kind of design or pattern may be made, either from whole moulds or by building up smaller ones. They can also be reduced in size by taking successive impressions and firing them: the jasper body loses one-eighth of its volume in the kiln. So the design of figures, leaves, scrolls, banded reeds or whatever can be lifted (or rather dropped) out of the mould and then luted, or applied to the surface of the ware by moistening with water.

This is an operation which calls for the greatest delicacy in handling, as will be obvious when one looks at the sometimes quite minute pieces of clay which make up these patterns. At this stage there is no difference in colour between the pieces of pottery and its applied relief: they are both a slatey-grey, rather like Plasticine. But as soon as the two have been fired the colouring oxides go to work, and the stained ground takes on one or other of the celebrated colours, leaving the relief to stand out in white.

CAMEOS AND MEDALLIONS

At first only smaller pieces were made, for Wedgwood still had many problems with larger pieces such as plaques and vases. The earliest jasper wares were mostly cameos and medallions in relief and seals in intaglio. Even these, however, could give trouble. Of the two blues, light and dark, the latter was the more saleable, but its disadvantage was that the stronger colour in the ground would 'bleed' into the delicate white cameo, sometimes with unhappy results. Wedgwood complained at one stage about what happened on one of the cameos to 'the poor Queen's nose'.

It was no easy task, either, to get thin pieces of clay—say $\frac{1}{16}$ to $\frac{1}{8}$ in. through—to stay flat and unwarped in the kiln and also keep its colour even and clear throughout at the high temperatures required for fine stoneware.

But Wedgwood was a tireless experimenter—there are over ten thousand trial pieces in various media at Barlaston today to bear witness to it—and as time went on he solved most of these difficulties. He learned, for example, to turn such problems as that of 'the poor Queen's nose' to advantage by working out designs which put the 'bleeding' to good use, for example by giving shading to a drapery, or 'turning away' a figure so as to make it seem to stand up in sharper relief.

HANDWORK ON THE RELIEFS

One of the chief factors in the high quality of the reliefs in the early wares was what was called the 'undercutting'. If you consider for a moment how the reliefs were made—by pressing clay into an open mould—it will be obvious that if the clay is to come out of this mould cleanly the mould cannot dig under an arm or a leg to make it stand out. Skilled workmen were therefore employed to cut away under these projections while the relief was 'leather hard', which accentuated lines, rounded off projections and thus heightened the relief. This detailed undercutting is, in fact, one of the tests for the early wares; they were made in days before it became prohibitively costly to employ on such work someone who had to have many of the qualities of a sculptor.

Blue jasper centrepiece, 9¼ ins. diameter, with applied yellow and white strapwork. The foot has a scroll and rope border and there are applied flowers inside the bowl. Marked 'WEDGWOOD'. *Etruria 1790.*

COLOURED GROUNDS

The first of the coloured grounds to be developed were the light and dark blues, both of them from cobalt. This is one of the limited number of pigments which take kindly to the high firing temperatures necessary for stoneware and porcelain. Shades could vary from something like indigo to a pale bluish lavender: on some of the early wares there is also a delightful soft grey-blue or slate colour.

Two or three shades of sage-green, also a colder blue, green, and a very rare olive-green were obtained by using cobalt and iron; while the attractive lilac colour, always a great favourite for ornamental wares, came from manganese oxide. This proved so fugitive a colour in the kiln, however, that a great many pieces came out as a brownish pink, or even a *café au lait* flushed with pink: in fact, Eliza Meteyard, Wedgwood's nineteenth-century biographer, called the colour 'peach-blossom'. Naturally its very variety has always charmed collectors, who welcome a warm hue among so many cold ones.

The jasper yellow, another very rare colour, is usually slightly greyish, sometimes with a touch of amber or even buff; but other specimens, the rarest of all jasper it is said,

(Right) *Flower-pot in tricolour jasper, with diced work and quatrefoils.*
(Below) *Bowl with flowing arabesque scrolls in relief.*

come out almost lemon-coloured. The black achieved in jasper is rich and glossy, slightly translucent, and quite different in hue from the black basaltes.

FORTUNATE ACCIDENTS

These differences in hue and tone, although prized by collectors, do not necessarily denote different classes of coloured jasper. William Burton, who was chemist at Etruria for five years in the late nineteenth century, has pointed out that many of them are due to variations in temperature or atmospheric conditions (actively oxidizing or reducing as the case may be) according to where the piece was standing in the oven. There was certainly every imaginable hue and tone among the hoard of trial pieces left by the first Josiah, who would have tried every possible variation he could.

All the same, if these colours were accidents, some of them were very happy ones, and their uniqueness and attractiveness not only adds to the fascination of collecting jasper ware, but also makes its mark in the saleroom.

Other colours were introduced in later years. Perhaps the most striking of them was the crimson which was used between 1910 and 1928. It was a bold venture, and seems to have been discontinued because—like the dark blue which did such dreadful things to the Queen in Josiah's day —the colour ran and turned the reliefs pink. During these years also the dark olive-green reappeared, together with a buff in 1929–33. A Royal Blue was created in 1953 to mark the Coronation of Queen Elizabeth II, for the tea wares mentioned on page 39, and also for boxes in various shapes and sweet-dishes.

There are many happy combinations of colours, sometimes on the larger pieces, but also on many of the smaller pieces for the boudoir, or to be worn as jewellery. Lilac is admirably used with green on cameos, and there is a handsome vase in the Schreiber Collection (Victoria & Albert Museum) with lilac and white reliefs on a buff ground.

Terracotta with white and also (for 'prestige' items) black jasper was made in small quantities from 1957 to 1959, while from 1929 to 1933 the firm made some bas-relief ware in buff jasper dip with black jasper reliefs. But the line was discontinued

White jasper vase with coffee-coloured arabesque scroll between olive-green and coffee borders, the cover surmounted by a sleeping child. 8½ ins. high. (Sotheby & Co.)

and sold off at the 'Century of Progress' Exhibition of Chicago. According to Mr Harry M. Buten these pieces are now much sought after, especially those not marked 'Made in England'.

Early oval and round medallions have quite a range of different colours, separately or in combination. Some are to be found with a dark olive-green ground, pale blue borders and white reliefs; another type will show a white relief on a pale green ground and also on a black border. Sometimes a border will be pierced, as with the popular creamware plates and dishes.

JASPER 'DIP'

In the early days of jasper ware the clay was coloured 'solid throughout' as we have seen from Josiah's description. But in a year or two there appeared a version in which the ground tint was produced by dipping the piece in colour. This is known as jasper 'dip', and after about 1780 its use became general except for quite small pieces. It has been claimed by some that this step was taken by Josiah because he wanted to economize on cobalt, but the process of 'dipping' cost him much more than solid jasper: he claimed that it would oblige him to raise his prices by twenty per cent. Solid jasper was not reintroduced until 1856.

Sometimes a body of one colour is 'dipped' in another, and the edges bevelled and polished so that the ground colour shows through, giving a three-colour piece. Or a white jasper body may have a wash or 'dip' of colour in front which differs from the blue at the back. A blue jasper 'dip' can be applied over solid blue, or the ornament applied to a jasper 'dip' body may be in solid coloured jasper. About 1820 there was a race of white jasper showing two- or three-colour reliefs. Light blue as well as lilac jasper were reintroduced in 1959 after a gap of many years.

STYLES OF DECORATION

Jasper ware is famous, of course, for the classical designs used in the reliefs, and we shall be discussing some of these later. But many people find no less attractive the other forms of decoration used on jasper ware, employing the same technique of raised reliefs, but giving quite different effects.

There is, for example, lattice work in relief, sometimes white on lilac. There is also the very handsome diced work. Here the ground is 'engine-turned' (Wedgwood was one of the first men in the Potteries to use machinery) and a chequer pattern created by cutting away the 'dip' in squares, alternate ones having applied quatrefoils in a third colour.

Equally effective is the strapwork technique, whereby a three-colour result is achieved by cutting and layering in lines. Both this and the diced work consort astonishingly well with modern ideas of decoration, and one wonders why they are not made again; presumably they were costly processes.

Even with ordinary reliefs, however, some very pleasing effects occur where the reliefs simply combine various decorative forms like acanthus, ivy and vine leaves, lilies, arabesques of flowers, reed and band flutings, Greek key patterns, and trailing roses. Such pieces are not only worth having in themselves, but are welcome additions to a collection of pieces showing the more conventional reliefs.

Another very interesting development in design occurred about the time of the Great Exhibition of 1851, when Wedgwoods, like many other potters, were making great use of themes taken directly from nature, for example, flowers and trailing plants. Both at this exhibition and the subsequent one in 1855 they showed several very handsome examples of this work in jasper ware, as is seen in our illustrations below.

Mid-Victorian jasper decorated with overall plant patterns: these styles appeared at the Great Exhibition of 1851, and the Paris Exhibition of 1885. (City of Portsmouth Art Gallery.)

3. Decorative and Ornamental

It was Josiah Wedgwood's proud boast that he could make jasper ware in all sizes from minute cameos, small enough for the smallest ring, to plaques suitable to cover a fireplace surround. There is even a mysterious reference in a Bristol newspaper in 1790 to a bridge of jasper ware over the Trent: it was reported as having been washed away in the winter floods.

But of all his wares he seems to have been proudest of his 'tablets'—we call them plaques—and his vases. They 'only want age' he prophetically wrote to Bentley, 'to make them valuable'.

Many of the plaques now treasured in the cabinets of collectors, or in frames upon their walls, were once part of the actual furniture fittings in eighteenth-century drawing-rooms, studios, or boudoirs. As can be seen on page 21 the larger oblong plaques could be built into mantelpiece or chimney-piece. Sometimes it was combined *en suite* with oval or round medallions on either side. The same plaques,

'Antonia with the Urn', a sacrifice subject, and *'Sacrifice to Hymen'*. All modelled by William Hackwood.

'Psyche Wounded and Bound by Cupids'. Dark blue jasper plaque or medallion, $4\frac{1}{2}$ ins. by $2\frac{3}{4}$ ins.

rectangular, oval, or round, would also be disposed around the room on wainscots, doors, or pilasters; they would appear as fittings on window shutters, bell pulls, even above your head on the ceiling—in the Buten Museum there is a ceiling fixture of jasper a foot in diameter with convex circular medallions.

Some of these fittings can still be seen in their original homes, notable at Osterley Park, Kedleston, Mellerstain, etc.

RARE EARLY PLAQUES

Plaques from the earliest days of jasper ware, the 'period of perfection' as it has been called, are and always have been extremely rare. Frederick Rathbone reckoned that even at the end of the last century—since when many must have been destroyed—all the known ones from the best period, say 1776 to 1795, could be arranged in three lines round an ordinary art gallery.

Even after Wedgwood was able to say of the smaller pieces that 'jasper is absolute', they certainly presented immense problems in firing. Long flat slabs, usually not more than a quarter-inch thick, were extraordinarily un-predictable in the oven, and it required the greatest care to avoid making them curl up in the heat. Their colours were also very tricky to manage. But all such difficulties only spurred the indefatigable Wedgwood on to greater efforts: all his lifetime he was seeking for better methods and more striking effects.

INSETS IN FURNITURE

Soon the plaques and medallions began to find their way on to movable furniture. Chests of drawers, cabinets, buffets, chairs, desks, bookcases, and tables would be inset with them: so would sewing boxes of rosewood and king-wood, sometimes with the medallions set in silver or gold, cut steel or ivory. At the Heritage Foundation, Deerfield, Mass., there is a grand piano by Broadwood (a firm which like Wedgwoods is still going strong) decorated with jasper ware cameos and Tassie gems. It was made to the order of Don Manuel de Godoy—'Prince of the Peace' as he was named by Napoleon and Prime Minister to Queen Maria Luisa of Spain, who gave it to him. It was sent out to Spain in the year 1796, costing with all its trimmings (including 'cartage to the key') the sum of £257 5s. 6d. After Godoy's fall it was taken to France, presumably as a piece of loot in the Peninsular War, and eventually found its way to the United States after being successively owned by two English collectors, Mr R. W. Hudson and the first Viscount Leverhulme.

Clocks, inkstands, and other items of the early days were inlaid with jasper medallions, and the process went on during the nineteenth century. There is a clock (see page 21) made by Vulliamy, the well-known London maker, called 'The Young Geographers', which has two jasper figures of boys holding compass and sextant. Three circular medallions of 'The Three Graces', 'A Warrior', and 'Apollo' in white relief on deep rose-coloured grounds are mounted on the pedestal, which also has finely chased ormolu. The

Fireplace surrounded with jasper plaques or 'tablets'. (Above) A mantel clock by Vulliamy of London, with two white biscuit figures of boy geographers, and cones, books, etc. in ormolu. A pink jasper oval medallion of 'Cupid as Summer' is mounted on the base.

medallions date from about 1790. Another generation of jasper decorates a clock with a black and white jasper face which was made by Reynoldson of Hull, Yorkshire, in 1860.

Items can also be found from countries which have imported Wedgwood cameos for insetting. One such is an inkstand in the Buten Museum which consists of a green 'dip' and white footed *cachepot* mounted in brass, with holders for seals, pens, paper; tapers, etc. It is impressed Wedgwood, but rubber stamped with a French mark of origin dating it to 1900.

But in late Victorian days almost everything could be given its Wedgwood additions. You could even buy coal scuttles with decorations of the famous relief of 'Hope Attended by Peace, Art, and Labour'.

EARLY VASES

As collectors' pieces it is probably the vases which have been most keenly sought after in the past, especially the spectacular ones from the early days. 'From the beginning,' wrote Wedgwood, 'I determined to spare neither time nor expense in modelling and finishing my ornaments, and I have the satisfaction to find that my plan has hitherto met with the approbation of my friends, and that purchasers of every nation declare them to be the highest finished and cheapest ornaments now made in Europe.'

The first outstanding success was the 'Homeric Vase' presented by Wedgwood to the British Museum, and still there. It was modelled by John Flaxman from a bell krater owned by Sir William Hamilton, husband of Nelson's Emma and a great collector. It is sometimes referred to as 'The Crowning of a Citharist', but Wedgwood himself called it 'The Apotheosis of Homer', on what grounds one does not know, although he meant it to represent the

Vase with reliefs of 'The Procession of the Deities', taken from the 'Puteal of the Twelve Gods', now in the Capitoline Museum, Rome. (Victoria & Albert Museum.)

deification of the poet. There is a companion vase called 'The Apotheosis of Virgil'. The 'Homeric Vase' was regarded by Wedgwood as being at that time 'the finest and most perfect I have ever made'. It is 18 ins. high and is in black jasper 'dip' with white reliefs.

Other famous vases included an amphora in pale blue jasper, 15¼ ins. high, with white reliefs of 'Apollo and the Nine Muses' on a granulated blue ground; the cover, like those of the two vases already mentioned, is surmounted by a Pegasus or flying horse in white jasper. These very large vases were not made—they could not have been—before about 1785 to 1790, and it must have been a source of great regret to Wedgwood that his partner Bentley did not live to see many of them.

At this time a great many smaller vases were turned out, and it is mostly these which appear in the salerooms today. They usually bear the same kinds of reliefs as the plaques and medallions, and there are often some odd juxtapositions. On one vase may be found trophies and weapons, and on its pair a replica of Sir Joshua Reynolds's 'The Infant Academy'; or Lady Diana Beauclerk's chubby little boys prancing on one side of a vase with 'Hercules in the Garden of the Hesperides' on the other.

Favourite designs for round vases were those which showed a procession of some sort, for they could be adapted to the length required. Flaxman's 'Dancing Hours' (see pages 26–7) was one of these.

THE PORTLAND VASE

But the most celebrated work of Wedgwood's in this field was his series of copies of the Portland, or Barberini, Vase.

This famous *objet d'art*, now in the British Museum, has had many romantic stories woven around it, involving Pope Urban VIII, the Roman Emperor Alexander Severus and even Alexander the Great. It was supposed to have carried the Emperor's ashes, and to have been found in his sarcophagus.

The known facts about it seem to be that in about the year 1780 it was in the possession of the Princess Barberini, who sold it to a Scottish gentleman named Byres. He in turn sold it to Sir William Hamilton for £1,000, who thought it to be a work of the time of Alexander the Great. Sir William sold it to the Duchess of Portland—making a profit of £800 in the process —and when the Duchess died soon afterwards it came up at the sale of her many works of art. Wedgwood sent his agent to bid for it, but the vase was bought in by the Duke of Portland; whereupon the master potter asked the Duke if he could borrow it to see if a copy could be made.

The practical Wedgwood soon discovered that instead of being made of onyx or chalcedony or some such hardstone, as all the connoisseurs had supposed, it was actually made of glass. It was in fact an outstanding example of

Jasper vase modelled by Hackwood in 1790, with reliefs of 'Venus in her Chariot', after the design by Vigée-Lebrun. A taste of rococo among all the neo-classical.

The 'Dancing Hours', first modelled by Flaxman, and later in this more draped version by Hackwood. These figures appear on many vases and plaques.

cameo glass cutting dating from about the first century B.C. The dark blue, almost black, body of the piece had been cased with an outer skin of white opaque enamel glass, the latter then being cut or carved away to make a design in relief.

PELEUS AND THETIS

The subject seems to be as obscure as the origin of the vase itself; but the most commonly accepted interpretation of the two scenes shown is that they illustrate the courtship of Peleus, a King of Thessaly, and Thetis, one of the Nereids. She was an Immortal, which Peleus, although grandson of Jupiter, was not. Because of this, Thetis rejected his advances, and to hide from him constantly changed herself into a bird, a tree, or a tigress. But Peleus invoked the aid of the gods, who suggested that his only course was to surprise her while she was asleep in her grotto near the shores of Thessaly.

Reproducing the vase in jasper ware was a fabulously difficult operation, and Wedgwood spent the better part of four years over it, employing William Hackwood and William Wood on the designs. The first 'edition' was ready by 1790 and a copy was shown to the public in the Wedg-

wood Showrooms in Greek Street, Soho, together with a certificate from Sir Joshua Reynolds, President of the Royal Academy, that it was 'a correct and faithful imitation, both in regard to the general effect, and the most minute detail of the parts'.

TODAY'S KNOWN COPIES

Wedgwood himself never stated the number of copies issued, but Wolf Mankowitz in his book *The Portland Vase and the Wedgwood Copies* has made an estimate. He reckons that assuming all the copies up to No. 15—the first 'good one', according to Wedgwood—were not destroyed as imperfect, there were about forty-five copies in the original black jasper, of which no more than thirty-one would have been of the finest quality.

None of these copies were marked, although some were numbered inside the lip in pencil. The list of those people who ordered copies still exists, and the known copies today total thirteen with numbers and six without. Examples may be seen in the British Museum and the Victoria and Albert Museum, London; the Wedgwood Museum at Barlaston; the Lady Lever Art Gallery, Port Sunlight; and the Fogg Museum, Cambridge, Mass.

Josiah Wedgwood's replica of the Portland or Barberini Vase, produced in 1790 after four years of trials. This copy is No. 12 of the first edition and was presented by Josiah Wedgwood to Dr Joseph Priestley.

During the first Josiah's lifetime another version was issued in solid blue jasper, and a copy of this edition stands alongside the first edition copy in the British Museum. The original was smashed by a neurotic young man named Lloyd in 1845 and (rather clumsily) repaired.

In the same case is a copy of the remarkable reproduction in glass made about 1873–77 by John Northwood, the famous Stourbridge glassmaker, using exactly the same carved cameo technique as the original, but on a transparent blue glass. Unfortunately it cracked in the carving. Northwood was also retained by Wedgwoods to 'polish' an edition of thirty copies, and the records show that at least fifteen copies were sold. They bear the initials 'JN' in cypher over the impress mark, and a copy stands in the Wedgwood Showrooms in London.

In early Victorian times, according to Mr Mankowitz, an edition was put out with the figures tactfully draped. It appeared with both a black and a blue ground, but the work is not so fine as in either the original or the later Northwood versions. Another issue was made for an American firm in 1909: and editions in various sizes (including miniatures) and in all the jasper colours have been issued by Wedgwoods from 1880 down to the present day.

JASPER FIGURES

Figures are not often found alone in jasper, though they are often mounted on other items like the candlesticks on page 32. Pegasus, the flying horse, is often met with on the lids of vases.

In plain white jasper there were portrait busts of Voltaire, Antony and Cleopatra, and other subjects; a later series made about 1860 after the sculptor Wyon has a rather coarser body.

Very few animals were made on their own: pug dogs and elephants are mentioned, but apparently not often seen.

The eighteenth-century world loved to fill its rooms with the colour and fragrance of flowers and foliage. Long before he came around to inventing his jasper ware, Wedgwood—like the other potters in Staffordshire and in the porcelain factories in England and on the Continent—was making *jardinières*, myrtle pans, orange tubs, bulb pots, bough pots, and other containers of the sort.

They appeared in most of other Wedgwood wares—black basaltes, rosso antico, creamware, cane or bamboo ware, and, of course, the famous green glazes. But a gathering of bulb and flower holders in jasper ware alone would stand up as a collection, and amply display all the various shapes and decorative techniques. Particular use was made of the attractive diced wares, especially in orange tubs. The basket-weave impressed pattern appeared on tall bough pots, while the three-coloured strapwork appears on many shapes. There is a blue and white open bowl with a continuous scroll of 'aquatic leafage' inside its rim which suggests its own use. A popular form was an oval bulb pot in solid blue jasper with foliate or figure reliefs and movable 'tree stump' fitments for growing living flowers in water.

RUSTIC AND ROMANTIC

In many of these pots—as in the 'rustic' candlesticks shown on page 32—Wedgwood reverted to the romantic forms of the rococo which he, like the rest of Staffordshire, had indulged in early in his career, but which with his neo-classical ideas he had done so much to destroy. The classical idea is never very far away, of course, and it comes out again in a short cylindrical vase, green or blue, with a white hexagonal plinth bearing reliefs of 'Blind Man's Buff' and a flat cover for the insertion of flowers. There is also a black jasper pot shaped like the plinth of a monument which can have alternatively a fitment with small holes for flowers or a 'tree trunk' bulb holder.

A romanticized version of the classical creeps in again with

Celadon green jasper jardinière, with loose cover and 'rustic' holders for four growing bulbs. White reliefs of 'The Nine Muses and Apollo'. 1790.

holders which are imitations of the 'romantic ruins' which gentlemen of the time were busily putting up in their grounds. They show truncated columns standing on battered plinths, and must have ravished readers of Maria Edgeworth's novels.

In Victorian times Wedgwoods produced round tapering pots in blue and white jasper as much as 16 ins. in height, with pierced linings so that they could be used for rooted plants; also a new orange tub design with applied reliefs.

LAMPS AND CANDLESTICKS

We do not perhaps realize today how much Georgian domestic life revolved around the lamp and the candlestick, so pleasantly throwing their soft light on silver and glass and mellow furniture. Pottery and porcelain makers joined the silversmiths very early on, and, as might be expected, Wedgwood was in the foreground again using all his various bodies.

In jasper, however, he found some difficulty: candlesticks had to be more massive than other items in the ware, which made them hard to manage in the kiln, so they are relatively rare. So, too, are the smaller tapersticks, with tiny socket holes wherein fragrant tapers stood to offer light for sealing-wax or pipe.

Among the candlestick shapes are the already mentioned pairs in 'rustic' style. There are Tritons in solid pale blue and white jasper, also modelled by John Flaxman; and the far more charming pair of children, 'Summer' and 'Winter', by William Hackwood, with white figures and foliage on a green tree trunk. The classical themes were used on the drums of candelabra: on the colour plate we show one of a pair from the Wedgwood Museum at Barlaston. They are 10 ins. high and the socket drip tray and lustres are in Waterford glass, the black and drums being mounted with ormolu. Strapwork decoration is featured in a pair of taper holders oviform in shape with a reversible lid: on one side is a figure, on the other the taper socket.

Wedgwood produced several lamp shapes adaptable to the newly patented Argand Lamp, which burnt colza oil and gave a more brilliant light than had ever been seen

'Rustic' candlesticks with figure of Cupids as 'Summer' and 'Winter', modelled by Hackwood in white, against a sage-green ground. 1784. 10 ins. high.

before; the potter drew attention to the 'singular and beautiful effect' of this on reliefs. He also followed the Greek or Roman hand-lamp, but this shape was adapted for pin trays, inkstands, or taper boxes.

Other items which might be found in eighteenth- and nineteenth-century rooms included a holder for the fumigated ribbon popular in Victorian times (in earlier days, of course, there had been pastille- or incense-burners which served the same purpose); jasper lions, which did duty as paperweights or bookends; and metal vases, which would sometimes have jasper reliefs let into them as did workboxes and other items of furniture.

JASPER CHESSMEN

Chess players will find it difficult to assemble a complete set of the famous chessmen modelled by Flaxman and made between 1783 and 1785. The major pieces are usually in white jasper on bases of blue or green; the pawns are usually also in blue or green. Here, for once, this neo-classical sculptor departed from his and Wedgwood's favourite period, for the pieces are in medieval costume, the pawns representing foot soldiers (halberdiers, bowmen) of the time; it is said that they represent the cast of *Macbeth*, with Mrs Siddons (playing Lady Macbeth) as the Queen. They were made in various jasper colours, including blue, olive green, and lilac.

Harry Barnard, who himself modelled a series in 'Flemish green' in 1926 (marked HB) says that 130 sets were made between 1785 and 1795; a new edition of Flaxman's set was issued in 1880 in black and cream Queensware.

A chessboard in the form of a circular table top in black and white jasper is spoken of by William Burton; he says it had motifs from a medieval tournament by the famous designer Walter Crane, associate of the Pre-Raphaelites, and was produced about 1870 for one of the international exhibitions. If so, it would have been a fitting setting for the famous chessmen. One wonders if the table still exists.

4. Tea and Table Ware

Some of the finest work on jasper went, strangely enough, into such 'useful wares' as the *déjeuner* set and other items for the table. It would probably be a mistake to think of these as any less 'ornamental' than Wedgwood's grander things, like the vases and plaques. They were clearly never meant for the rough and tumble of daily use; and if they were used at all, it was only on important occasions.

The largest single groups were the 'Tea and Coffee Equipages', which usually consisted of a tea and/or chocolate pot, sugar box, cream jug, two cups and saucers, and a tray large enough to take them all. This latter was probably the most difficult of all the pieces to make because of the customary trouble in firing large flat pieces of jasper ware.

But extraordinarily careful work went into even the tea

Jasper déjeuner *set, with reliefs of 'Domestic Employment' and 'Poor Maria' designed by Lady Templetown and modelled by William Hackwood.*

cups—sometimes, by the way, handle-less like the porcelain ones from China and Worcester. Usually only the outsides of the vessels were 'dipped', the insides being left white and not glazed but polished, like the edges of some of the medallions. Because of this they are translucent, like porcelain, and in one of the catalogues Wedgwood took care to have one engraved in such a way as to show this quality, of which he was very proud. Many pieces bear the mark—presumably a workman's—'O' or '3' or both together.

DECORATED TEA WARE

The decoration of some of these sets is quite enchanting. They often feature the pretty diced pattern with quatrefoil

'No. 129'

JASPER COFFEE WARE

'Boston'

'Pear'

'London'

35

Tea caddy

Preserve jar

'No. 146'

Butter lugger

Biscuit jar

'Brewster'

'St Louis'

TEA CUPS

'Pear'   'Brewster'   'Bute' (footed)   'Bute'

37

JASPER JUGS

(Above) '*Orange*'; '*Etruscan*'
(Below) '*Dutch*'; '*Bentley*'

ornaments, graduated in size and radiating from a centre. Sometimes there is a reserved panel, but instead of the expected relief of figures there will be a monogram of the owner's initials. Around it will run the acanthus leaf, the flowing Vitruvian scroll, Greek key patterns, and the rest. Most of the jasper colours are called into use, and in some cases there are cans and saucers in white jasper with borders of ivy leaf in green with berries in pink; others will have a green ground with blue and white diced bands mounted with green quatrefoils. Many of the designs do not seem to have been used for other wares, and one rarely sees a defective piece.

When figures are used with reliefs they are often the subjects associated with Lady Templetown, Lady Diana Beauclerk, or Sir Joshua Reynolds's 'The Infant Academy', all highly suitable for my lady's boudoir.

JASPER JUGS

(Above) '*Byerley*'; *Metal mount*
(Below) *Covered upright; Upright*

In this same class will be found plates and dishes, salt-cellars, butter dishes, centrepieces, tea measures, custard sets and caddy spoons. Trays can be oval, square, or round, with fluted and engine-turned decoration. Mr Gladstone had one with a slate-blue ground and white reliefs and quatrefoils.

Modern jasper ware also offers some collectable items in tea services. There is the one already mentioned, made in a limited edition in Royal Blue jasper to commemorate the Coronation of Queen Elizabeth II—it bears the profile portraits of the Queen and the Duke of Edinburgh. This in itself makes it a rarity, for Royal portraits may not be used on wares for more than six months after a permitted occasion.

5. Toilette and Trinkets

Jasper wares offered themselves in all kinds of ways for the toilet table. There were toilet boxes 'to hold pins, patches, pomations, rouge, gloves and bows, tassels, gold and silver ornaments, lace, buckles, rings and knick-knacks'.

The little shaped black patches used in those days for hiding a blemish on the cheek and imparting a sparkle to the eye were kept in oblong boxes, $3\frac{1}{2}$ to $4\frac{1}{2}$ ins. long, and here jasper cameos were used in combination with all kinds of materials. The box itself might be made of ivory with a cameo of the 'Vestal Virgin' set in a plaque of cobalt-blue glass; or perhaps in a framework of cut-steel beads or a gilt frame. On one of these the jasper is in lilac, blue, and white, and the lining inside is of crimson velvet. There are also wooden patch boxes with the cameos set in several ways.

Scent or 'smelling' bottles came in a variety of shapes in whole jasper, as will be seen from the illustrations, or in cut-glass with a blue and white cameo. Some had a relief on either side, pairing, for example, the Prince of Wales and the Duke of York; the King and Queen of England; Henry IV of France and the Duc de Sully; and famous ladies like the Princesse de Lamballe and the Duchess of Devonshire. For bluestockings there was a bottle with Rousseau on one side and Voltaire on the other.

JASPER JEWELLERY

Ladies and gentlemen could also carry the famous cameos in all kinds of ways about their persons, whether 'at home or abroad'. Cut-steel jewellery, manufactured by people like Matthew Boulton of Birmingham, was in its heyday then, and all manner of brooches were made up in it, and set with jasper cameos. There were clasps, buckles, brooches, seals, and chains.

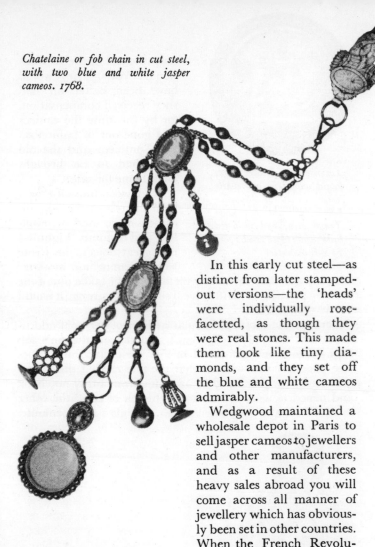

In this early cut steel—as distinct from later stamped-out versions—the 'heads' were individually rose-facetted, as though they were real stones. This made them look like tiny diamonds, and they set off the blue and white cameos admirably.

Wedgwood maintained a wholesale depot in Paris to sell jasper cameos to jewellers and other manufacturers, and as a result of these heavy sales abroad you will come across all manner of jewellery which has obviously been set in other countries. When the French Revolution broke out the firm lost touch with these stocks, and did not find them again

Tortoiseshell powder box, inlaid with blue and white jasper cameo of 'Sportive Love', designed by Lady Templetown, and modelled by William Hackwood. 1786. 2¼ ins. diameter.

until the end of the Revolutionary Wars. They would have been better off had they received compensation, for by this time the cameos had gone out of fashion on the Continent and the old stock had to be brought back home for sale.

Wedgwood himself took a keen interest in the way his cameos were used in jewellery and costume. 'Lightness is a great object,' he wrote to his Birmingham mounter in 1786, 'and therefore if any metal could be taken out of the back by piercing . . . and leave it sufficiently strong, it would be an advantage.'

Perhaps the most spectacular articles of personal adornment was the lady's chatelaine and the gentleman's fob chain. From our picture of one of these elaborate pieces (see page 41) you will see that the one carried the ladies' 'necessities', which could be anything from a tiny notebook and pencil to a scent bottle or a bunch of keys; the other usually held the gentlemen's seals, eye glass and penknife.

Cut-glass scent bottle set with black and white jasper medallions with subjects by Lady Templetown. 1785.

42

Wooden patch box inset with cut-steel beads and a blue and white jasper cameo by Lady Diana Beauclerk. 1786. There is a mirror inside the lid and the box is lined with cream-coloured velvet. 1786.

As well as this the well-dressed man might carry one or more cameos on the hilt or scabbard of his sword or dagger, and another on the handle of his walking stick. His watch case might carry a cameo with a very tiny one on the key. At the opera he would peer through a 'monocular' or single eye glass with a jasper case, take out a snuffbox inset with a cameo, and look down to see one on the buckles of his shoes and the pin to his cloak.

A century later, when the pipe-smoker had replaced the snuff-taker, he could buy a head of jasper ware ('Staithes Patent') and mount a reed in it; if he wanted to paint a picture he could take with him into the park a complete set of paints in a jasper ware box. For Oriental gentlemen there were hookah vases and 'chibouques'—whatever they were—mounted in silver and gilt metal.

The lady, for her part, would most likely have had a cameo locket on her breast, on her hairpin, on her finger rings, scarf and hat pins. In recent years cameos have even appeared on the heels of shoes, marketed in the United States by Clemans at 49 dollars 50 cents a pair!

Lady's shoe with heel of blue and white jasper. Made for H. & M. Rayne. 1959.

43

6. Cameos and Medallions

As we have seen, Wedgwood's own taste, especially after his meeting with Bentley, was for the historical and classical themes which were in his day not merely a fashion but an obsession with the nobility and gentry. Great collectors like the Dukes of Northumberland and Marlborough, Sir William Hamilton, Sir Watkin Williams Wynne, and Sir Roger Newdigate, brought back with them from their treasure-seeking tours among the art dealers and noble homes of Europe carved or engraved gems, 'Etruscan' vases, busts of marble or bronze, as well as many books of engravings of famous tombs and other monuments.

Everyone who couldn't afford an original wanted copies of such relics of the newly discovered past. They were in the market for replicas of gems in glass paste or any other suitable material, for plaster casts of stone busts and statues, reliefs and other works, all to adorn their new Adam-style houses—with which they were in perfect harmony.

Earliest examples were the cameos and medallions in relief and the seals in intaglios; until then they were only in white biscuit, black basaltes, and the first 'waxen' jasper.

Wedgwood himself never seems to have distinguished between cameos and medallions, or between medallions and plaques, but Miss Meteyard and others have proposed that a cameo measures up to, say, $2\frac{1}{2}$ ins., beyond which it is a medallion; one might suggest that anything over about 6 ins. is a plaque—what Wedgwood called a 'tablet'.

PORTRAITS IN POTTERY

In the beginning Wedgwood had to buy many of the designs used for the cameos and intaglios, especially the portraits. Some he had as sulphur casts from James Tassie, the celebrated Scottish modeller in opaque glass paste, who ran a thriving business copying items borrowed from the cabinets and galleries of most of the important European collectors. Raspe's catalogue of his work, published in 1790, credits Tassie with having produced no fewer than 15,800 different subjects. Tassie's portraits are admirably done. Also they are named, which has been a great help to their many ardent connoisseurs down the years.

But Wedgwood did not long remain a customer of Tassie's. He objected to paying out money for them—one invoice shows that he bought seventy for twopence each. Perhaps Tassie himself began to see little sense in supplying so formidable a competitor with cheap designs, especially as the Wedgwood & Bentley Catalogue went out of its way to claim that their stoneware cameos were finer than those in any other material—presumably including glass.

So Wedgwood began to build up a connexion of his own with collectors, and also gathered round him a team of modellers who were capable of either turning out original work or adapting the designs sent in by others.

THE 1779 CATALOGUE

Perhaps the most helpful way of classifying the subjects of these reliefs and intaglios is Wedgwood's own, as shown in the 1779 Wedgwood & Bentley Catalogue. Here, Class I covered 1,735 cameos and 739 intaglios 'exactly taken from the finest gems'. The intaglios were often polished, especially where the subject was a head, when the fine blue jasper was given 'as good a polish as turquoise stone or Lapis Lazuli'. The subjects included 'Egyptian History, Gods and Goddesses, Sacrifices, etc., Philosophers, Poets and Orators; Kings of Macedonia, etc.; Fabulous Age of the Greeks; The War of Troy, Roman History, Masks, Chymeras, etc.; Illustrious Men', and an Appendix covering an assortment of items ranging from 'A Crouching Venus' to Pope Clement XIV, and from George III to 'an Egyptian figure covered with hieroglyphicks.'

In Class II of the Catalogue are the 'bas-reliefs, medallions, cameo-medallions, tablets', etc., totalling

(Above) *William Pitt.*
(Below) *Sir William Hamilton*
(*the impressed name can just be seen*).

222 subjects, while Class III embraces 'Kings and Illustrious Persons of Asia, Egypt and Greece'.

Here Wedgwood was obviously setting his sights at the neophyte collector, for he described this as a 'Biographic Catalogue of distinguished characters, for the Illustration of that pleasing and instructive branch of History. . . . Besides an extensive mythological Cabinet, we can furnish a suite of *Grecian* and *Roman* History, from the Time of the *Trojan War* to the Removal of the Seat of the *Roman* Empire to *Constantinople.*' He goes on to say that 'the thread of history is continued by a set of the *Popes* near *compleat*, and all the Kings of *England* and *France*; and the more present periods of History are illustrated by a considerable number of *Poets*, *Painters* and other famous persons, from *Chaucer* to the present time'.

In this section the subjects included 'Kings and Queens of Asia Minor, Greece, etc., Statesmen, Philosophers and Orators of Greece, Poets,

Grecian Heads of Large Models'.

In other classes there was a series of sixty medals from Dassier, illustrating Roman history from the foundation of the city to the end of the Consular government; heads of illustrious Romans, of the Popes, Kings of England and France, and of 'Illustrious Moderns from Chaucer to the present time'—that is to say Wedgwood's time.

ILLUSTRIOUS MODERNS

These are of the greatest interest today, and by some good judges have been classed as probably Wedgwood's most important work artistically. Many of the earlier 'moderns'—Chaucer, Gower, the Elizabethans, and others—were largely imaginary, but with those of Wedgwood's own day enormous pains were taken to get good likenesses, either by using paintings or sculptures or by modelling the subjects direct from life.

Without these cameos we would not have had likenesses of many of Wedgwood's more distinguished contemporaries They included

(Above) *Sappho.*
(Below) *Marie-Antoinette.*

47

famous seamen, explorers, and soldiers like Captain Cook, General Monk, Warren Hastings, Admirals Hood and Keppel, distinguished personages like David Garrick and Sarah Siddons, Sir Joshua Reynolds the painter, Dr Johnson, William Pitt, scientists like Sir Isaac Newton and Sir William Herschel, as well as Royal and noble personages from Britain, France, Italy, Germany, Russia, and other European countries.

EARLY AMERICAN

Among these 'moderns' are a number of famous figures in United States history. Benjamin Franklin and his son and grandson appear on portrait medallions dating even from before the War of Independence, while after it came portraits of Washington, Lafayette, Paul Jones, and William Penn.

This reflected a profoundly critical attitude to his own government in the matter of the dispute with the American colonists. He subscribed anonymously to funds for American prisoners of war taken at sea and he was prophetic enough to write on one occasion: 'I tell them, the Americans will make laws for themselves, and if we continue our Policy— for us too in a very short time. . . .' In another place he wrote: 'In continuing the relationship of child and parent as applied to British and America we were obliged to acknow-

(Above right) *Anti-slavery medallion, designed by Josiah Wedgwood and adopted as the seal of the Slave Emancipation Society.*

(Left) *One of a pair of blue and white jasper 'dip' plaques representing the destruction of the Bastille by figures with pick-axes, commemorating the fall of the Bastille. The first shows the crowd breaking into the prison and raising the tricolour; the second shows figures on the battlements breaking them down with pick-axes.* (Sotheby & Co.)

ledge the disagreeable facts that we have driven out the brat in his infancy, and reposed him in an uncultured forest to the mercy of wild beasts and savages, without any further enquiries after him till we imagine he might be brought to render us some essential services. We then took him again under our parental protection; provided him with a straight waistcoat,

and whenever he wriggled or winced drew it up a hole tighter and behaved so like a stepmother to our son, now grown a very tall boy, that he determined to strip his waistcoat and put on the toga at once.'

According to another letter, all these jasper wares included a portion of Cherokee clay from South Carolina, so it seems some of these early portrait medallions of American leaders have in them a piece of the United States itself.

The portrait medallions of all types were originally sold in sets, and sometimes in handsome mahogany cabinets. In these the collector gathered together his groups of illustrious personages from all times and countries.

PORTRAITS TO ORDER

But in making his portrait medallions Wedgwood by no means confined himself to the illustrious. In the catalogue he 'begs leave in this place to observe that if Gentlemen or Ladies choose to have models of themselves, Families or Friends, made in Wax, or engraven in Stones, of proper Sizes for Seals, Rings, Lockets, or Bracelets, they may have as many durable Copies of these models as they please, either in Cameo or Intaglio, for any of the above Purposes at a moderate Expense. Copies of cameos and intaglios for rings could be had for five shillings apiece, for bracelets, seven shillings and sixpence each.'

In a later catalogue he advises patrons to have their portraits modelled in wax by Joachim Smith, who would charge them three guineas for an original of the size suitable for a ring seal or bracelets and five guineas for one making a medallion three to five inches in diameter.

Whole families sat for their portraits in this way. Some of them, like those of Lady Finch and her daughters, were, although commissioned privately, bought in jasper copies by the public simply because it was charmed by the subject. Many of these sitters have still to be identified—which offers a perpetual quest for the collector of jasper ware.

There were also many subjects not appearing in the catalogues, including figures associated with the wars between France and the German States. These were made for export, so there may still be some discoveries to be made here.

Sometimes a cameo has an intaglio on the reverse, or there may be double cameos or double intaglios mounted back to back. One shows George III on one side and Queen Charlotte on the other. The metalworkers seem to have initiated this idea by mounting unrelated ones thus.

The original sets of intaglios were impressed with the number as well as the name of the subject, so they are easily recognized. Many have the ground polished, leaving the figure untouched; with shank seals, the shank was polished as well as the bevel. Some had blue jasper grounds, making them look like the banded onyx used for seal cuttings.

TOPICAL THEMES

As one might expect from a man who kept himself so up to date in world affairs, Wedgwood was swift to commemorate events as they occurred. The Bastille fell on 14th July 1789 at the beginning of the French Revolution; by the 24th Josiah Wedgwood II wrote to his father: 'Do you think it would be proper to get some snuffbox tops with the Duke of Orleans' head on them. . . . You will no doubt

'Priam begging for the body of Hector from Achilles'. Modelled in Rome by Pacetti.

have seen in the papers that the French have recovered their liberty and that the Duke is a great favourite with the popular party.' By the 28th, Wedgwood senior had portraits in hand both of Orléans and of Necker and Mirabeau.

Popular themes of the day inspired other cameos. There are two subjects from Goethe's *Sorrows of Werther*, which is almost a textbook of the Romantic Movement. One of them is 'Charlotte Mourning at the Tomb of Werther'.

The 'Botany Bay Medallion', made from clay brought home from Australia, commemorates the landing there; the Jacobite Cause is marked by a cameo of Prince Charles Edward, the Young Pretender.

Wedgwood was also a keen supporter of the Anti-Slavery Committee and a generous subscriber to its funds. At his behest Hackwood modelled for him a cameo (see page 49) showing a slave kneeling in chains with the inscription: 'Am I not a man and a brother?'

Wedgwood had thousands of these medallions made and distributed them free to anyone who wished to use them as anti-slavery propaganda. A letter exists from Benjamin Franklin, who had received a free parcel for distribution in the newly independent United States, thanking Wedgwood for them and saying he thought they might have an effect 'equivalent to the best-written pamphlet'. These little cameos were mounted as hat pins, buttons, rings, etc. 'Thus', wrote a member of the Committee, 'fashion which usually confines itself to worthless things, was seen for once

'Friendship Consoling Affliction'. Designed and adapted by Lady Temple-town from a bas-relief in the Louvre.

in the honourable office of promoting the cause of justice, humanity and freedom.' The original issue of this cameo was unmarked, but later editions bear the potter's name.

CLASSICAL SCENES AND CHARACTERS
Collectors have found endless interest in the scenes from classical mythology, and many of those made by the early designers are still in demand today.

The story of the Trojan War is told in one series, beginning with the birth of the Greek hero Achilles ('The Childbed of Thetis').

The next scene shows Thetis dipping her son into the protective waters of the River Styx, but fatally covering with her hand the heel which was afterwards to prove the hero's vulnerable point. Then one sees her delivering the boy to the mother or sister of Cheiron, the learned centaur; after which he appears as a young man at the Court of Lycomodes, the King of Skyros, whence he had been sent disguised as a girl by his mother, to avoid the campaign against Troy. Apparently he lived for some years undiscovered among the daughters of Lycomodes, until his unmasking by Ulysses. As shown in another relief this wily sailor-hero came to Skyros disguised as a pedlar, selling women's clothes and fairings.

Among these he had concealed some weapons and armour, and when he sounded a trumpet call, Achilles took up the weapons and so betrayed himself.

Then follows a scene from the Trojan War itself when Achilles, furious and distraught from the death of his friend Patroclus, overcame Hector and dragged the fallen Trojan's body behind his chariot three times round the walls of Troy, under the eyes of Hector's father King Priam.

Jupiter sent a message to Priam encouraging the old man to go to Achilles and beg from him the body of Hector, so as to remedy the disgrace by giving him a formal funeral Facing almost certain death, Priam went to the Greek tents accompanied only by another old man like himself.

In the relief illustrating this event (see page 51) one sees Achilles still mourning the loss of his friend, Priam kneeling at his feet, Mercury who had been sent by Jupiter to conduct Priam safely to the rendezvous, and wagons containing the tribute which was being offered for the release of the body, which had been protected from harm by the gods. Achilles, moved by the entreaties of the old man, who had now lost the mainstay of his kingdom, granted the request, 'and peaceful slept the mighty Hector's shade'. These scenes are taken from a marble disk in the Capitoline Museum in Rome.

Another incident in the war is shown in the 'Sacrifice of Iphigenia'. Agamemnon, the Greek leader, who was preparing the fleet for the expedition to Troy, happened while out hunting to kill a stag which was sacred to Diana. Calchas, the soothsayer, said that the goddess would have to be appeased or the Greek force would be wiped out by a pestilence; and insisted that only the sacrifice of a virgin, in fact Agamemnon's daughter Iphigenia, would satisfy Diana. All was arranged for the sacrifice, but at the last moment the chaste moon goddess relented, and leaving a hind in place of the maiden, whisked her off to Tauris, where she was made a priestess of Diana's temple.

Diana herself, under her Greek name, figures in various

53

subjects concerning the young shepherd Endymion, who spent his night sitting under the moon on Mount Latmos. Jupiter had made him the gift of eternal youth, and Diana, entranced by his beauty, came down to visit him every night: but protected her modesty by having him also blessed with the gift of eternal sleep. In one medallion we see his dog trying to wake him at the approach of the moon goddess; in another, he appears in a group asleep with his head on an old man's lap. Diana is being led by a Cupid or Eros, and this pair often appeared as decorative motifs on their own, especially in the well-known 'Offering to Peace'.

Bacchus or Dionysus, the god of wine, appears in various reliefs. He was the son of Jupiter by Semele, a fact of which his wife Juno was extremely jealous. She thereupon conceived a plan whereby Semele could be destroyed by Jupiter himself. Taking the form of an old nurse, she sowed doubts in Semele's mind whether it was in fact Jupiter who came to her as a lover, and suggested that the girl could only put her mind at rest by insisting on Jupiter appearing in his full immortal splendour as the first of the gods.

Semele first persuaded Jupiter to make an irrevocable oath to do whatever she wishes, and then asked him to appear as Juno had suggested. He did so, knowing what would happen, but having no alternative; and the mortal maiden was reduced to ashes. Jupiter then took her son, the infant Bacchus, and put him in the care of the Nysæan nymphs, who as their reward were placed among the stars as the Hyades. In the relief 'The Birth of Bacchus', the baby god is being delivered to the nymphs by Hermes, or Mercury; and the Wedgwood design for this was taken from a marble vase found at Cormia on the Gulf of Gaeta.

Bacchus discovered the secret of cultivating the vine, but Juno had him driven mad and he spent many years wandering about the earth. When he returned to his native Thebes, the people gave him a great triumph—which also appears as a subject in Wedgwood plaques, in a version from the Borghese Vase, now in the Louvre.

The labours of Hercules, brought upon his head as another outbreak of jealousy on the part of Juno—he was the son of Jupiter by Alcmena—appear in the reliefs. He is often seen as a single figure strangling the Nemean lion; he also appears in a more elaborate subject in 'Hercules in the Garden of the Hesperides'. These were the daughters of Atlas, who bore the weight of the world on his back, and Hercules had been sent there to find the golden apples which Juno had received at her wedding: the goddess had entrusted them to the Hesperides, assisted by a watchful dragon. Hercules overcame the dragon but had no success with the daughters, so he approached Atlas and offered to relieve him of his intolerable burden for a while if he would go and fetch the apples. Asking the old man to give him a cap to make the job more comfortable, Hercules managed to snatch the apples away and bear them off to Olympus. The subject was taken from one of the vases owned by Sir William Hamilton, and now in the British Museum.

Perhaps no subject has been so popular down the years, nor so often repeated, as the 'Marriage of Cupid and Psyche' (see below). Here they are represented in a charming way as babies, both veiled and lead by a rope: Psyche's wings are those of the butterfly, symbol of the soul, while Cupid

'Marriage of Cupid and Psyche'. Modelled by Flaxman after an antique gem, and used for all kinds of jasper pieces.

55

Kings and Queens from a jasper ware chess set designed and modelled by John Flaxman in 1783–5. (Sotheby & Co.)

kisses a dove. The procession is headed by a Cupid with a bow and brought up by one bearing a basket of fruit. This subject is thought to have dated from classical times, but some hold that it was taken from a Renaissance sardonyx now in the Boston Museum of Fine Arts.

Another favourite is 'Psyche Wounded and Bound by Cupids' (see page 19). In Wedgwood's version, taken from one of the books, the figures have been carefully draped in the Etruria fashion. 'Venus and Cupid', which shows the goddess holding a spray of four flowers, two of which droop down to the head of the little boy, is apparently a single subject taken from a carnelian.

In some cases a totally inappropriate title has fixed itself on to a relief. The so-called 'Sacrifice to Hymen', in which Cupids play music and dance, is, according to Dr Macht, from a cinerary urn now in the Capitoline Museum, and represents either a miniature thiasus, or a symbol of life after death. In the same way the subject called 'Friendship Consoling Affliction' (see page 52) by Mrs Landre seems to have been adapted from a bas-relief in the Louvre called 'The New Bride': the only difference appears to be that the weeping lady is now having water poured over her feet, whereas in the original she was having them sponged.

The famous 'Dancing Hours' (see pages 26–7) is one of the

figures from the same source as 'The Triumph of Bacchus' already mentioned; it seems to have undergone a transformation even after it was first issued from Etruria. The first version, by Flaxman, follows the original fairly closely; but later Wedgwood got Hackwood to do a less pagan version with more drapery, and this is the one we know.

Pomonax, goddess of fruit cultivation and especially of the apple orchard, is often seen; and so is Flora, goddess of flowers, who was loved by Zephyrus, the gentle west wind.

On very small cameos one often sees 'Demeter Searching for Persephone', where the corn goddess, carrying her scythe, is seen holding in her outstretched hand a torch. She wandered day and night looking for her daughter, who had been taken down to his dark kingdom by Pluto. Eventually Demeter did succeed in finding her daughter, but was allowed to see her only for six months in a year.

'Bellerophon Watering Pegasus' is another long-standing favourite since it was first made in 1773. The winged horse Pegasus was produced from the blood which sank into the earth when Perseus cut off Medusa's head. Minerva caught the horse and gave him to the Muses (who are also seen in reliefs watering him); when Bellerophon was required to destroy the monster Chimæra, he was given a golden bridle so that he could catch the horse and vanquish the monster.

ARTISTS AND MODELLERS

Wedgwood employed many artists directly and indirectly, but perhaps the most famous of them was John Flaxman. Flaxman, who was about twenty years old when

Blue and white jasper teapot with relief of 'The Infant Academy' by Sir Joshua Reynolds.

57

jasper ware came into being, had studied at the Royal Academy where he won two prizes. He has sometimes been confused with his father, who had the same Christian name, and whose name appears on Wedgwood invoices; but it now appears that Flaxman senior was a maker of plaster models from the antique, who supplied Wedgwood with models.

John Flaxman was responsible for some of the most famous of the designs put out from Etruria, and although Wedgwood at one time called him a 'coxcomb' he later came to regard him as one of the greatest artists of the age.

Not a great deal of Flaxman's work can positively be identified. He did some of the more famous of the plaques, including 'The Birth of Bacchus', and the 'Muses', also the first and now apparently lost version of the 'Dancing Hours'. There was also 'Mercury Joining the Hands of France and England', a perennial favourite, and of course Wedgwood's chief pride, the 'Homeric Vase'. Flaxman was elected an Associate of the Royal Academy in 1797; his monuments of Reynolds, Nelson, and Howe are in St Paul's Cathedral.

Many of the models were obtained from Rome. In 1787 Flaxman went there and set up a studio where he not only worked himself, but hired Italian artists to copy from the wealth of antiquities there. The names of these artists are known but they can rarely be associated with particular pieces, for these were usually thoroughly worked over at Etruria and made to conform to the general style.

Wedgwood himself was a skilled modeller in his early days, and even at the height of his fame and prosperity would sometimes bear a hand with the work. It appears from one letter that he worked on the busts of both Voltaire and Rousseau. He inspected designs and had the smallest things in them altered when they didn't please; he was also constantly having old models improved in workmanship.

In 1769 Wedgwood told Bentley that he had hired 'an ingenious boy' for modelling work at Etruria. This was William Hackwood, who was to work there for the next forty years and turn out a whole range of pieces of every

kind which are now avidly sought by collectors. Hackwood
worked on a great many of the portraits: outstanding ones
are several of George III and Queen Charlotte, two of
Shakespeare, one of Wedgwood himself, and another (one
of the very finest), a study of an old bricklayer at Etruria
named Edward Bourne. He also made many medallions,
and his large tablets include 'The Birth of Bacchus' and the
revised version of the 'Dancing Hours'. It also seems a fair
inference, as he was then senior modeller at Etruria, that he
was responsible for the Portland Vase figures. Webber, who
▓▓▓▓▓ ▓▓▓ ▓▓▓▓▓▓▓▓ ▓▓ ▓ ▓▓▓▓▓ ▓▓▓▓▓▓▓▓ ▓▓▓▓▓▓▓▓ ▓▓▓
two charming candelabra 'Diana' and 'Minerva'.

Among the many other names recorded, few of which can
positively be identified as to their work, are Denby and Boot.

LADY DESIGNERS
Wedgwood also used designs by Society ladies like Lady
Diana Beauclerk, Lady Templetown, and Miss Crewe. They
were usually charming little domestic scenes and infant
bacchanalia, and appear a great deal on the 'tea equipages'.
They were and always have been tremendously popular, as
Wedgwood knew they would be. When he received the first
of the drawings from Lady Templetown he was careful to
send them along by his nephew, together with an effusive
letter asking for more—which was, as usual, successful.

Not all these designs were original: in fact probably most
were adapted from the antique. As we have seen, 'Friendship
Consoling Affliction' is from a plaque in the Louvre.

Marks on Jasper Ware

WEDGWOOD

Wedgwood

Used in various sizes from 1759 to 1769 and again from 1780 (after Bentley's death) to the present day. The word 'England' is added on export wares made after 1891 to comply with the American Customs Regulation known as the McKinley Tariff Act. See also the date marks in use until 1928 and the numeral letters in use from 1929 onwards (see page 62).

Wedgwood &
Bentley

Used on Wedgwood & Bentley intaglios 1769–80, with a catalogue number varying in size.

W. & B.

Very small intaglios were sometimes marked thus, with the catalogue number, or sometimes with the number only.

Rare mark found only on chocolate and white seal intaglios, of 1769–80 era, usually portraits made of two layers of clay with the edges polished for mounting.

WEDGWOOD & SONS

Very rare mark used for a short period in 1790—according to Rathbone on large square plateaux in cane-coloured jasper. It may have been intended for use at the change of partnership, when Wedgwood brought his sons into the business after Bentley's death.

WEDGWOOD
ETRURIA

Wedgwood
Etruria

Said to have been used on pieces of a very high character about 1840.

O 3	Found upon jasper *déjeuner* services of the early period, sometimes with the numeral only. Supposed by Miss Meteyard to be the mark of a particular workman.
L. Tub E. Wash TBO	Marks used on experimental pieces, making reference to technical matters. TBO, for example, can indicate 'top of the biscuit oven'.
Wedgwood & Co.	Mark of Ralph Wedgwood of the Hill Works, Burslem, and Ferrybridge, Yorkshire, a relative of Josiah Wedgwood. Used until 1800.
Wedgwood & Co. Ltd.	Used from 1840 to the present day by the firm of Wedgwood & Co. Ltd., Tunstall, Stoke-on-Trent.
WEDGEWOOD	Mark of William Smith & Co., Stockton-on-Tees, Yorkshire, from 1826. An injunction was granted against this firm at the instance of Josiah Wedgwood & Sons.
WEDGWOOD	Sometimes found on jasper ware of continental manufacture.

Note: Jasper ware will also be found unmarked, or with the marks of other manufacturers. These include John Turner of Lane End; William Adams of Greengates; Humphrey Palmer and his partners and successors at the Church Works, Hanley (Neale & Co.; Neale & Wilson; Wilson); Samuel Hollins of Shelton; John Adams & Co., and Adams & Bromley of the Victoria Works, Hanley; E. J. Birch of Shelton; W. T. Copeland & Sons; Enoch Wood of Burslem. The firm of Dudson Bros. Ltd produced a variation on blue jasper with a glaze.

Abbott & Mist is thought by Geoffrey Godden (*British Pottery and Porcelain*) to be the mark of the London selling agent for John Turner.

Jasper ware has also been imitated in porcelain in Paris, Meissen, Vienna, Doccia, and Ilmenau.

Date Marks

In 1860 Wedgwood introduced a system of date marking in addition to the trade mark. These date marks consisted of three capital letters: the first indicating the month, the second being the potter's mark, and the third the year in which the piece was made.

The monthly marks from 1860 to 1864 are as follows:

January	J	April	A	July	V	October	O
February	F	May	Y	August	W	November	N
March	M	June	T	September	S	December	D

From 1864 to 1907 these monthly marks were changed to the following:

January	J	April	A	July	L	October	O
February	F	May	M	August	W	November	N
March	R	June	T	September	S	December	D

The yearly marks from 1860 to 1930 ran in three cycles beginning with the letter O for 1860 and continuing through the alphabet in sequence to Z for 1871.

A second cycle began with A for 1872 and went to Z for 1897.

A third cycle started with A for 1898 to Z for 1923.

During this third cycle (in 1907) a figure indicating the cycle was substituted for the letter denoting the month since up to this point it was difficult to determine whether a piece was made in the first, second, or third cycle without consulting pattern or shape books or by other circumstantial evidence, as the following example points out:

Month	Potter	Year	
V	X	O	July 1860 (the beginning of date marking first cycle)
L	X	S	July 1864 (at the change of the code letter for months)
L	X	S	July 1890 (note the second cycle appears the same as the first)
Cycle			
3	X	J	1907 (a number denoting the cycle substituted for monthly mark)
3	X	S	1916 (1916 being the year S in the third cycle)

This confusing system of dating was discontinued in 1930. From that date a number designates the month in chronological sequence. A letter gives the potter's mark and the last two numbers give the actual year. For example:

Month	Potter	Year	
7	X	30	July 1930
7	X	32	July 1932
7	X	47	July 1947

X has been used to indicate the potter throughout this explanation. There have been many potters with their letters changing from time to time and assigned to others at the end of their term of service.

Registry Marks

From 1842 to 1883 when the British Patent Office employed a Registry Mark on English manufactured goods, Wedgwood used the mark in addition to the trade mark along with other manufacturers which indicated that the design was registered in the British Patent Office. When this mark appears it is possible to tell the exact year, month, and date of an object by using the following table.

Index to the Letters for Each Month and Year from 1842 to 1867

Year		Month	
1842	X	January	C
1843	H	February	G
1844	C	March 1845	W
1845	A	April	H
1846	I	May	E
1847	F	June	M
1848	U	July	I
1849	S	August	R
1850	V	September	D
1851	P	October	B
1852	D	November	K
1853	Y	December	A
1854	J		
1855	E		
1856	L		

23rd May 1842

1857	K
1858	B
1859	M
1860	Z
1861	R
1862	O
1863	G
1864	N
1865	W
1866	Q
1867	T

Letter R used from 1st to 19th September 1857.

December 1860, Letter K used.

Index to the Letters for Each Month and Year from 1868 (when Registry Mark changed) to 1883

Year		Month	
1868	X	January	C
1869	H	February	G
1870	C	March	W
1871	A	April	H
1872	I	May	E
1873	F	June	M
1874	U	July	I
1875	S	August	R
1876	V	September	D
1877	P	October	B
1878	D	November	K
1879	Y	December	A
1880	J		
1881	E		
1882	L		
1883	K		

CLASS
DATE
PARCEL
R^d
YEAR
MONTH